THE ITCHY KIDS CLUB
Silly poems for itchy kids

By Jill Grabowski
Illustrated by Max and Elena Stasyuk

Copyright© 2009, The Itchy Kids Club, LLC

ISBN: 1-4392-4913-X

THE
ITCHY KIDS
CLUB

WWW.ITCHYKIDSCLUB.COM

Thank you to my husband, Bob, and my wonderful family for their inspiration, support, and patience. And thank you to my itchy kids, Hannah and Francie, for making my life complete. Frustration fuels creativity. It is my wish and the wish of every itchy family that all itchy kids may one day find relief from their pain, discomfort, and fear.

And special thanks and a big "woo hoo!" to the incredibly knowledgeable and caring staff at National Jewish Health in Denver, Colorado. Before our two-week adventure, Francie had not had an itch-free day or slept an entire night since she was first born.

This book is for all of you itchy kids in the world, both big and small. Don't let the itchiness get you down!

TABLE OF CONTENTS

Hey, What's an Itchy Kid?

An itchy kid is someone with allergies. If you have allergies, you know how uncomfortable they can make your body. They can make you itchy inside your stomach, in your eyes, on your skin, in your mouth ... ugh! I'm itchy just thinking about it.

What Is a Food Allergy?

ITCHY-TIP: When you see a word in bold, check the **vocabulary section** for a definition

Some kids are allergic to cats and dogs. Some kids are allergic to grass and pollen. Some kids are allergic to bee stings, latex, even medicines. And some kids are allergic to foods, like peanuts, fish, and eggs.

What's an allergy, you ask? **Allergies** are caused by your **immune system**, or the group of tissues and cells and stuff inside your body that protects you from diseases that can make you sick. The immune system acts like a strong army, surrounding, attacking, and killing any viruses, bacteria, or bugs (not the creepy crawly kind!) that try to get into your body.

When you have an allergic reaction, the immune system gets confused and attacks something that really isn't harmful to you. Like, say you're allergic to pollen. If you sniff some pollen in the air, your body will react by attacking it and releasing **histamines**, which will make you **itchy**. And if your immune system attacks something once, it always remembers it as an **allergen**, or an enemy, when it's really not. It will continue to attack the allergen every time it comes near your body. So, every time your body smells that pollen in the air (or touches an animal you are allergic to, or steps on grass, or swallows a peanut), your body will freak out and start attacking it, just like it did the first time. Your body will get sneezy, wheezy, runny, itchy, and miserable. Sometimes, your immune system gets so mad that it makes your body shut out all chances of getting another sniff or bite of the allergen. This is serious, as it causes an **anaphylactic** reaction. When this happens, you can get very sick. You break out in an itchy, splotchy rash; your throat feels scratchy; your breathing gets wheezy; and you might feel like you have to throw up or poop (yikes!). When this happens, it's time to grab that EpiPen and call 911!

Some really common things you may be allergic to are pollen (tiny little seeds blowing around in the air); mold; dust; animals; household cleaners and other stinky, strong chemicals; medicines; bug bites and stings; and certain foods—generally not peas or broccoli, so don't even try it! A lot of people who have allergies also have a skin problem called **eczema**. Eczema is a very itchy, red rash. Imagine having a bunch of mosquito bites on your arm that will not stop itching no matter how much or how hard you scratch; that's what eczema feels like. Some people get an eczema **flare up** from allergies, and some people break out when they are tired, hot, angry, or stressed. Their skin is so sensitive that they may have to use special soaps and lotions to try to get it to stop itching and to make the swelling go down. There is no cure for eczema, and sometimes it is very hard to control. Other common and sometimes serious reactions to allergies that you may experience are **asthma**, **hives**, and **hay fever**.

The most common food allergens are milk, eggs, peanuts, tree nuts, soy, wheat, fish, and shellfish. Other food allergens include meat, fruit, veggies, grains, and seeds. Lucky for most kids, food allergies are outgrown by the time they are five. Some kids, however, do not outgrow them.

Important Itchy Tip:

Kids with allergies, especially food allergies, should be tested at the doctor each year to see if their allergies have become any better or any worse. Your doctor (allergist) can help you to put an action plan together for you, your family, your doctors, and your school so everyone will know what to do in order to prevent a reaction, and what to do just in case a reaction happens.

Got eczema itchies? Research wet wraps at National Jewish Health in Denver, Colorado: www.nationaljewish.org. It's a simple process, and it has given us amazing results.

For more information and helpful and fun links, visit our website at www.itchykidsclub.com.

THE ITCHY KIDS CLUB

Francie is an itchy kid
Who loves to dance and sing
She plays with friends and goes to school
But there is just one thing

Francie has some allergies
To fish and nuts and stuff
And if she eats them by mistake
Her face will itch and puff.

See, some kids have a crooked toe
And some have curly hair
Some kids sneeze from dogs and cats
Or itch from things they wear

Everyone is different
With lots of funny traits
Allergies are one of them
That most kids really hate

Francie's body gets confused
And thinks some foods cause harm
And when she is around these things
Her brain sounds an alarm

It tells her body to beware
Then does some crazy stuff
Like make her sneeze and wheeze a lot
Or make her face puff up

Then she has to get a shot
From her EpiPen
It's a special plastic tube
Filled up with medicine

Francie has to keep her pens
At home and also at school
So that her teachers, mom, and dad
Can always keep their cool

Now you know why itchy kids
Must always watch their food
And you can help when they forget
Say, "Hey! Don't eat that, dude!"

Francie and her itchy friends
Need you to spread the word
How allergies can be a pain
'Cause many haven't heard!

And now you are a member, too
Of our Itchy Kids Club flock
Not because   you have allergies
It's just because   you rock !

HANNAH'S PET

Hannah had a little cat
Whose coat was black and white
But when she tried to pet his fur
Her skin became a fright

Itchy, icky, big ol' bumps
From head to little toe
Red and swollen achy lumps
Came fast but would not go

Poor Hannah had to give her cat
To Grandma to care for
Kitty could not stay with her
Not now, not anymore

Hannah cried for days and days
Thought she could feel no worse
Then mom came home from work one day
With a gift inside her purse

It was tiny, so warm and cute
His fur was curly and white
Hannah cried big happy tears
And hugged that puppy tight

"He's a poodle," said Hannah's mom
"His fur won't make you scratch!"
Curly was the name she chose
And it was a perfect match!

They never left each other's side
Little Hannah and her puppy
Kitty stayed at grandma's house
And they all felt very lucky

EATING BUGS

One day I tried to eat a bug
And it made my belly sick
But it didn't make my skin break out
Or make my lips all big!

See, I'm allergic to lots of stuff
Apples, meat, and fish
Milk and soy and nuts and wheat
But broccoli, nope (I wish!)

So I was happy to eat that bug
Cause I didn't have a reaction
I didn't itch or scratch a lot
Much to my satisfaction.

When you have allergies its kinda tough
Cause you don't have a choice
You must make sure that grown-ups know
You're not just making noise

Use your voice to let them know
How serious it can be
We have to get the word out quick
To this we all agree!

MY BABY SISTER

My baby sister can't have milk
Or soy or peanut butter
It makes her sick and itchy now
It even makes her shudder

At first I didn't like my sister
She's so small and cute
My mom and dad always tickle her
and laugh when she lets out a toot!

"It's not fair!" I yell and scream
Cause she doesn't pick up her toys.
It makes me cry when I have to share
It makes me mad, oh boy!

But then she got real sick one day
And we all got very scared
She cried and cried from tummy aches
And her skin began to flare

Mom took her to the allergist
Who did some prickly test
He told us what she could not eat
And to what we could say, "Yes!"

And now I have an important job
Cause I'm her only big brother
I must protect her from bad foods
And tell her that I love her

Tap! Tap!

LEARN TO SAY NO

Some people think it's rude to say
"No thanks!" when someone offers
Some snacks or juice or fruit to you
But really, it's not that awful

Some people don't know you can't eat
So many different foods
But if you tell them all up front
It won't be attitude

They need to know you can get sick
By eating the wrong thing
And don't want you to risk it all
Just so you fit in

So don't be shy and not speak up
For It could hurt you so
And people want to help you out
And they'd really like to know

WOE IS ME

My toes are itchy from the grass
My belly hurts from all the gas
My skin is tender from the rash
My hives are lumpy and aghast

Allergies from grass and trees
Belly aches from milk and cheese
Eczema from head to knees
Breakouts from food allergies

I don't like being such a pain
I don't like having to complain
But you must know how I disdain
These allergies make me insane

GLUTEN

Gluten is a protein that is
Used in rolls and bread
Many people are allergic
And break out when they're fed

Anything with wheat in it
Or rye or barley or oats
They get real tired and have some pains
And their bellies sometimes bloat

So they can buy some stuff without
Gluten for their meals
The organic store has lots of foods
That truly do appeal

To all who suffer and those who don't
These foods are sure to be tasty
Try to stop eating rye and wheat
And your skin won't be so pasty!

THE ALLERGIST

Every year I dread this day
and each time I complain
Cause it's the day that I find out
Which allergies remain

Once a year we have this visit
To the allergist I go
Then she pricks me on my arms
Until the bumps all show

Will I have more? Will I have less?
Only time will tell
Will it still be peanut butter
that makes my belly swell?

All I know is I see bumps,
All up and down my arm
Doc says I still got allergies
To lots of things; oh darn!

Guess its one more year again
Of being extra careful
And there's no use in being mad
In fact, I must be cheerful

It could be worse, I tell myself
I must agree to that
I could have lots more allergies
That I must combat.

BiG WORDS

My skin breaks out from eczema
And shrimps cause anaphylaxis
My mom gives me antihistamine
Which sometimes make me gaseous

Although I'm very young and small
And can't yet spell these words
I know firsthand what they all mean
Which may seem quite absurd

You see, I have food allergies
Which make my skin break out
And also make my throat close up
And lower lip pop out

So if you want to talk to me
Don't treat me like a baby
Cause I know lots of doctor words
And understand them all; well, maybe …

SO EMBARRASSING

My allergies are such a pain
I hate them oh so much
I don't break out from eggs or milk
Like other kids, as such

Hives would be a big relief
Instead of what I do
Each time I eat an egg or cheese
I have to poo and poo

I wish I had the itchy skin
Or bumpy hives instead
But when I eat a piece of cake
It's poopin' that I dread

When I can't resist that cheese
Or something with an egg
I get an achy pain inside
In my belly and down my leg

So off I run 'fore it's too late
To relieve my agony
It's my own fault, I know this now
And I need the will, you see

If I can just avoid those foods
I know it would be better
I could dodge that potty jail
And wouldn't be such a fretter

FRANCIE

There once was a girl named Francie
Who could never eat anything fancy
For each time she tried
She'd break out in hives
And itch from her shirt to her panties

ITCHY

I once
Tried to eat
Cheese but I broke out in
Hives and
Yikes! Had to sneeze

TARTAR SAUCE

I wish I could eat tartar sauce
On top of yummy fish, of course
But fish will make me sick or worse
So I'll just have some thick bratwurst

STINKY TOES

My toes are stinky
and smell like cheese
I must wear socks
Up to my knees

Spring or summer
When it's hot
I have to wear them
For what I got

Itchy legs and
Itchy feet
It makes me crabby
In this heat

But I need socks
To cover my skin
Cause if I don't
The hives begin

And though I hate
That sweaty smell
I cannot stand
When my feet swell

If I step on
Grass or mulch
My feet and legs
Begin to bulge

My allergies
Are so severe
I have to wear
These socks in fear

They keep the stuff
That makes me scratch
Away from any
Itchy patch

That's covered by
My big white sox
It looks like I have
Chicken pox!

I can't wait till
The fall is here
Then I won't have to
Live in fear

I'll wear long pants
And cover up
Those icky crusty patches
Yuck!

WHY!

Why oh why can't I eat dairy?
Why does it hurt me so?
Why does it make my tummy churn?
Why does it make me go?

How can something so very yummy
Make me sick and burn my tummy
Yogurt, cheese, and milkshakes, too
It makes me mad and sad, boo hoo

GREASY

Yucky, slippery, icky, and gooey
I hate daily bath time ... fooey!

Twice a day I get this bath
I soak in icky stuff
It helps the boo boos on my skin
And makes it not so rough

Eczema is what I've got
It's itchy and makes me bleed
I scratch some spots so hard sometimes
It makes my mom get peeved

So then she puts me in that tub
With special salt and oils
It calms my skin and itchiness
But smells like dead gargoyles!

I wish it didn't itch so much
And that I could have soap
In my bathtub every day
And then I wouldn't mope

SCRATCH-A-LOT-AY

Itchy, itchy, scratch-a-lot-ay
My skin looks all polka-dot-ay
I can't stand this itching all day
Want this stuff to go away, hey!

Scratching while I sleep at night
Makes me sore and real uptight
Even when the sun is bright
I feel like I just wanna fight

Allergies that make me crazy
I watch my foods; I can't be lazy
Smell the rose but not the daisy
If I do it makes me hazy

I wish I had just one or few
Instead of more than twenty two!
Take precautions, I daily do
To keep me from the hives and 'choos

iTCHY!

Itchy, itchy, I'm so itchy
But I cannot cry
My mommy told me not to eat it
And I cannot lie

It looked so yummy, it smelled so fresh
I could not pass it by
I stuck my finger in that cake
And licked it with a sigh

So now I'm itchy in my mouth
And also in my eye
I have to find my mom real quick
I think I'm gonna cry

It's not worth it, I don't think
To get one lick, oh my
cause now I'm scared I'm gonna puke
right on my daddy's tie

COUNTING POLLEN

In school we learned our ABCs
and then we learned our 123s.
I learned to count way up to thousands
But now, I have to count those pollens!

When the air is filled with seeds
It gets real hard for me to breathe
So when the news says pollen's high
I have to stay inside and cry

I don't know how they go about it
Counting all those tiny tidbits.
They must sit high up in a tree
Counting all the blooms they see

And then they yell to folks below
"It's fine today; the pollen's low"
Then Mom says it's okay to play
In my backyard with friends today

PB&J

Peanut butter makes me sick
So swollen that I can't breathe
My tongue swells up and blocks my throat
I can't even see my teeth!

I have to use my EpiPen
To shoot myself in the thigh
The needle itself is very small
And doesn't make me cry

I try real hard to stay away
From nuts and peanut butter
Just the thought of getting sick
Makes me shake and shudder

Sometimes people just don't know
That I cannot eat nuts
And they don't know how sick I get
I feel like such a klutz

I wish I didn't have to be
Such a royal pain to others
I hate that I have to ask all the time
"Is that made with peanut butter?"

At least I'm not the only one
I know there are so many
Who can't eat nuts or fish or beef
Like my friends, Bill and Benny

It gives me comfort when we eat
Our lunches at our own table
We never worry about sharing food
Or having to read every label

So if you feel like you are different
Don't worry, there are others
Just like me and my cool friends
Who can't eat peanut butter

NO MORE FISH

Please don't give me any fish
It makes my lips swell up and itch
Not just shrimp or crab, you know
I can't have trout or filet of sole

My mom said I am so allergic
I shouldn't even have a goldfish
A joke, perhaps, but I'm not sure
So to be safe I'll listen to her!

Cause every time I have a reaction
My mom and dad get really scared, and
They chase me with that EpiPen
And I have to get a shot again.

So please don't think me to be rude
But I don't want any stinky seafood
Fish sticks, crab legs, lobster, gumbo
Poppers, roughy, shrimps o' jumbo

All I want is to live peaceful
And no more shots would make me thankful
Give me chicken, turkey, and steak
All these things for me are great

Thanks for listening and paying attention
And now I must be sure to mention
If you see me nearing fish
Yell out loud and take my dish!

i THINK ALLERGIES STINK

Isabelle is always itchy
Tyler's tummy aches
Hannah can't eat fish and chips
Ingrid can't have cakes

Nina knows she can't eat nuts
Kaylee can't cut meat
Andy's allergies hurt his guts
Lynn's got swollen feet

Lana learned to watch her foods
Erin eats carefully, too
Rachel watches out for them
Gill helps his friend Lou

Ike has itchy, swollen eyes
Evie can't eat eggs
Sammy swells from head to toe
Sue gets bumpy legs

Tina tries to tame her hives
Isa gets irritated
Nicky's never tasted milk
Kevin's lips are inflated

All these kids have allergies
And know what they must do
If they need help when something's wrong,
 It's up to me and you.

Think of someone in your class
Who can't do all you do
And ask them what can bother them
From allergies and food

It's nice to be there to help out
When someone slips and falls
It's also nice to watch your friends
When allergies come to call

If you see them red and bumpy
And itchy from head to toe
Get a grown-up and yell real loud
To help your friend in woe

Don't be scared, 'cause it's okay
Your friends will be so glad
That you were there to help them out
When their allergies were so bad

ITCHY-LICIOUS

I may not be the top dawg, y'all
Or hoppin' through the grass
I may not be a flower child,
But I'm full of spice and sass!

My allergies to dogs and bugs
And grass and flowers and stuff
Can put a damper on my fun
And make me huff and puff

But that's okay, because I know that
This is just one thing
The rest of me is super hot
I'm phat, I'm cool, bling bling!

You can't let things hold you back
From being who you are
Just cause you've got allergies
Doesn't mean you can't go far

I'm itchy-licious; I got so much
To show this great big world
So stand back, folks, and let me through
I'm going places, girl!

VOCABULARY

Action Plan: A documented plan you and your allergist put together that should help you recognize your allergy symptoms, provide helpful tips on preventing allergic reactions, and give you information on over-the-counter and prescription treatment options should an allergic reaction occur. This plan should be shared with your family, friends, doctors, and teachers/school.

Allergen: A substance, such as a type of food or something that you can inhale or touch, that causes your body to think it is being attacked. Your body responds with an allergic reaction.

Allergic: The term used to describe you when your body is sensitive to harmless substances.

Anaphylaxis: Also referred to as anaphylactic shock, this is a very serious allergic reaction that may be life-threatening to you if you have severe allergies.

Anti-Histamine: A drug you can take to counteract the symptoms of an allergy attack.

Asthma: A disease of the airways in which certain things (allergens, cold or hot weather, even stress) can cause you to have problems breathing. Your airways become irritated or inflamed (swollen), and the air you try to breath has difficulty passing through.

Atopic Dermatitis: Eczema is a type of atopic dermatitis. This is a skin condition that many kids with allergies (and some without) have. It is an unbelievably itchy, crusty rash that appears when you have been exposed to an allergen or your skin has touched or been exposed to an allergen.

Eczema: See Atopic Dermatitis.

EpiPen: A plastic tube that contains a shot with epinephrine (a medicine used to stop a severe anaphylactic/ allergic reaction) in it.

Flare-Up: A term used to describe when your skin gets red, itchy, and irritated from an allergen.

Food Allergies: A condition that you have when your body/immune system is exposed to a certain food and you react to it.

Hay Fever: The itchy eye, runny nose, sneezy, and wheezy reaction to hay (not really a fever!) and other common irritants, such as flowers, pollen, trees that bloom in a certain season.

Histamines: This is the substance that your body releases when it thinks it is being attacked, and it will cause you to have an allergic reaction.

Hives: Also called urlticaria, these are itchy red bumps that appear on your skin after exposure to or ingestion of an allergen.

Immune System: This includes the group of tissues, cells, and organs in your body that work together to prevent and heal illnesses and even diseases.

Latex: A kind of rubber commonly used in clothing and gloves that many people are allergic to.

Prick Test: The allergist will prick your skin lightly with common allergens to see if your body responds with itchy hives, which means you are allergic to to that substance.

Wet Wraps: Used in the "Soak and Seal" process at National Jewish Health in Denver, Colorado, for the treatment of atopic dermatitis (eczema).

Made in the USA
Lexington, KY
06 May 2010